Silver Moon Above

I0502822

Passionate Heart Below

Original Landscape Arts

By

Aditya Kumar Daga

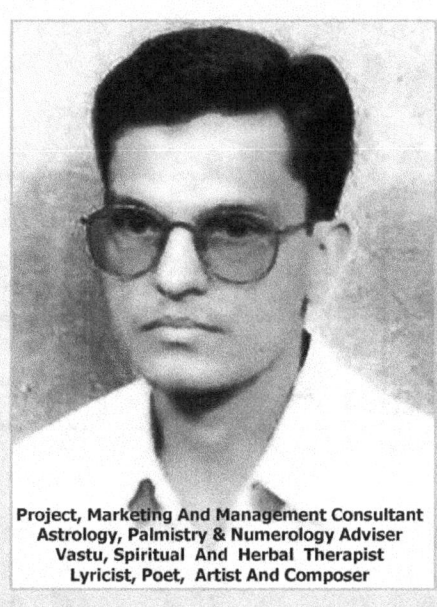

Project, Marketing And Management Consultant
Astrology, Palmistry & Numerology Adviser
Vastu, Spiritual And Herbal Therapist
Lyricist, Poet, Artist And Composer

Silver Moon Above

Passionate Heart Below

Dedicated To All

Who were a part of
My Passionate
Heart & Soul

Silver Moon Above
Passionate Heart Below

Copyright@ 2016 by Aditya Kumar Daga
All right reserved. No Part of this publication may be produced or reproduced or transmitted in any form or by any means, electronic or mechanical, including photocopy, or through any storage and retrieval system without permission from the Writer & author of the book Aditya Kumar Daga Lyricist, Poet & Artist

Published Through Create Space United States
In October 20 2016 as First Edition

All correspondences shall be made at
Aditya Kumar Daga
3C Gopi Bose Lane, Kolkata—700012 West Bengal India,
+919432221255; +91 8961429776
adityaastroworld@gmail.com
Www.adityaastroworld.com
Www.adityaartworld.com

PREFACE

Silver Moon Above
    Passionate heart below
        Hold me in your Arms
            Let my beats be slow

My dear do you know
    Why I miss you so
        Silver Moon Above
            Passionate Heart Below.

Let me tell you tale
    Unabridged   detail
        Why I think of you
            Like a drop of dew.

Droplets on the leaves
    Raining on the mists
        A flow of parting lips
            Pacing pulse on wrists.

Quickening Quivering feets
    Let my throbbing slow
        Silver Moon Above
            Passionate Heart Below.

Dark of raven nights
    Fear of deep ravines
        I am raving wild
            On this silver shines.

Silver Moon Above
    Passionate heart below
        Hold me in your arms
            Let my trembles slow.

PREFACE (Contd.)

Like a ton of fogs
    In the heart of clouds
        Wailing winds such songs
            Ravening moving sounds.

Shattering morbid mind
    Raining hard through eyes
        Searching you my love
            In Every waves of cries.

Silver Moon Above
    Passionate heart below
        Hold me in your arms
            Let my beats be slow.

Winds are sizzling loud
    Light is crossing cloud
        Dark is getting wild
            Drenching clumps around.

My soul is searching past
    My heart is loosing hold
        A fear I never knew
            Get my nerves so cold.

Flaking waves of light
    Flashing Dusky night
        Out of parting clouds
            Moon get silver bright.

Silver Moon Above
    Passionate heart below
        Hold me in your arms
            Let my nerves get slow.

PREFACE (Contd.)

In such flashing light
  On such silver sight
    I always get confused
      Flagged-n-slowly drooped.

A veil of haze up high
  Sheathing up sky
    Piercing in my nerves
      Jerks of lonely lurch.

Silver Moon Above
  Passionate heart below
    Take me in your arms
      Let my pulse be slow.

In that humid vast
  I get maddening fast
    Flash too short-n-curt
      A vacuum in my heart.

How I long to chase
  Night is full of craze
    Meteors getting frost
      Will-o'-the wisp & lost.

An Ever candid touch
  Exploding in me much
    First forever kiss
      All immortal wish.

Piercing through spine
  Tingling like a pine
    Losing hold on breathe
      Cracking underneath.

Silver   Moon   Above
    Passionate heart below
        Hold me in your arms
            Let my beats be slow.

By
Aditya Kumar Daga

Original Arts On Landscape follows

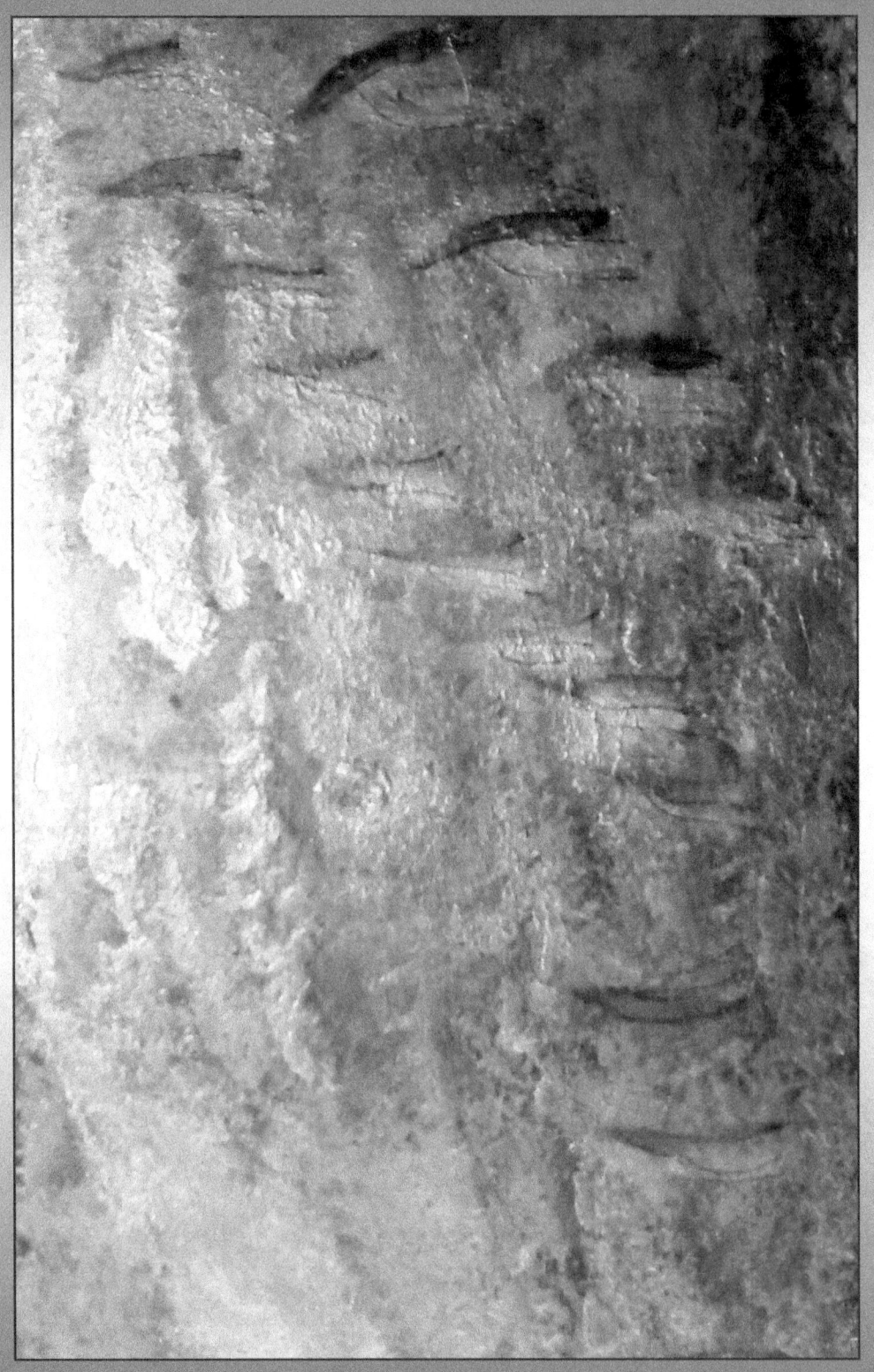

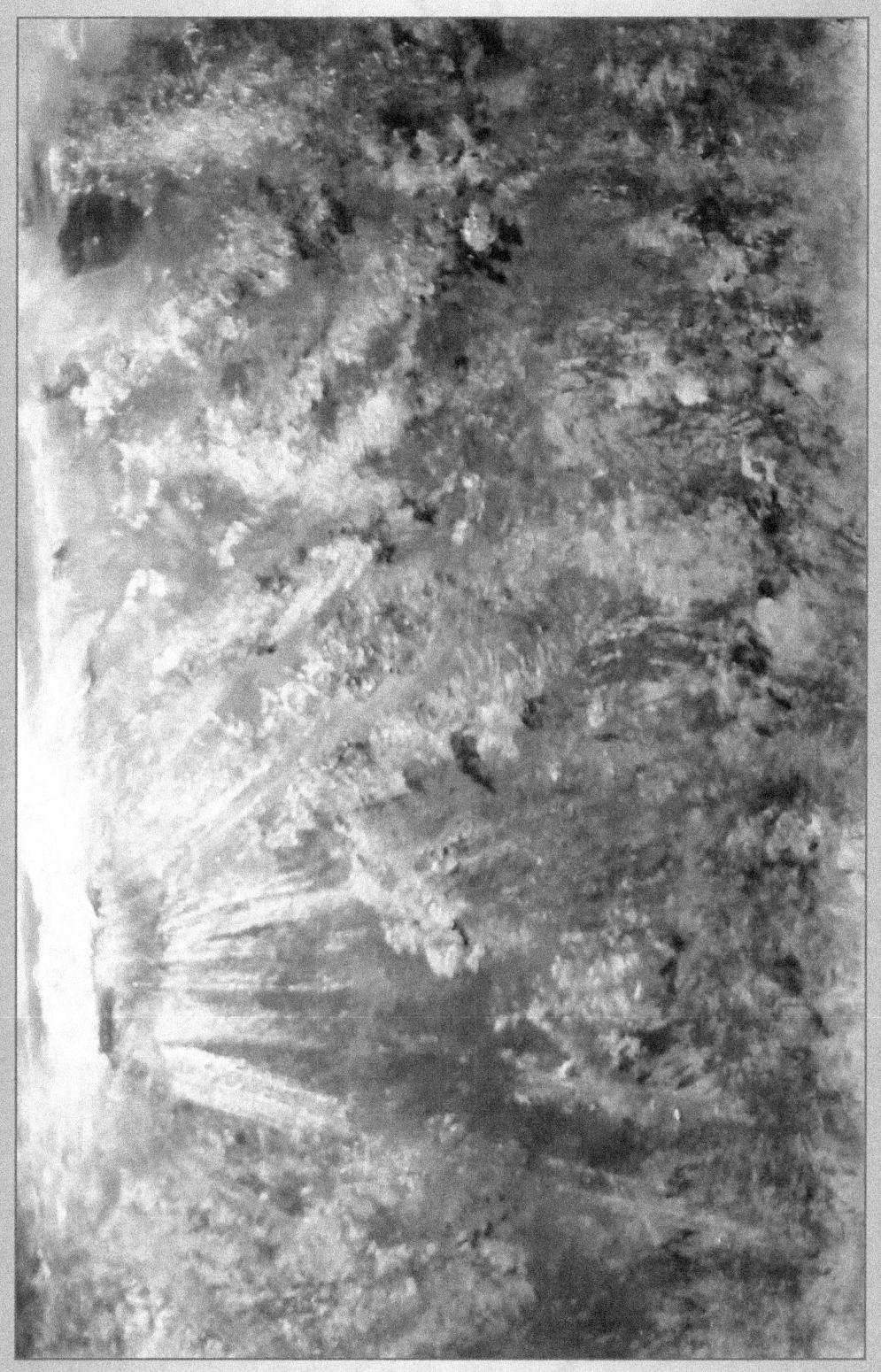

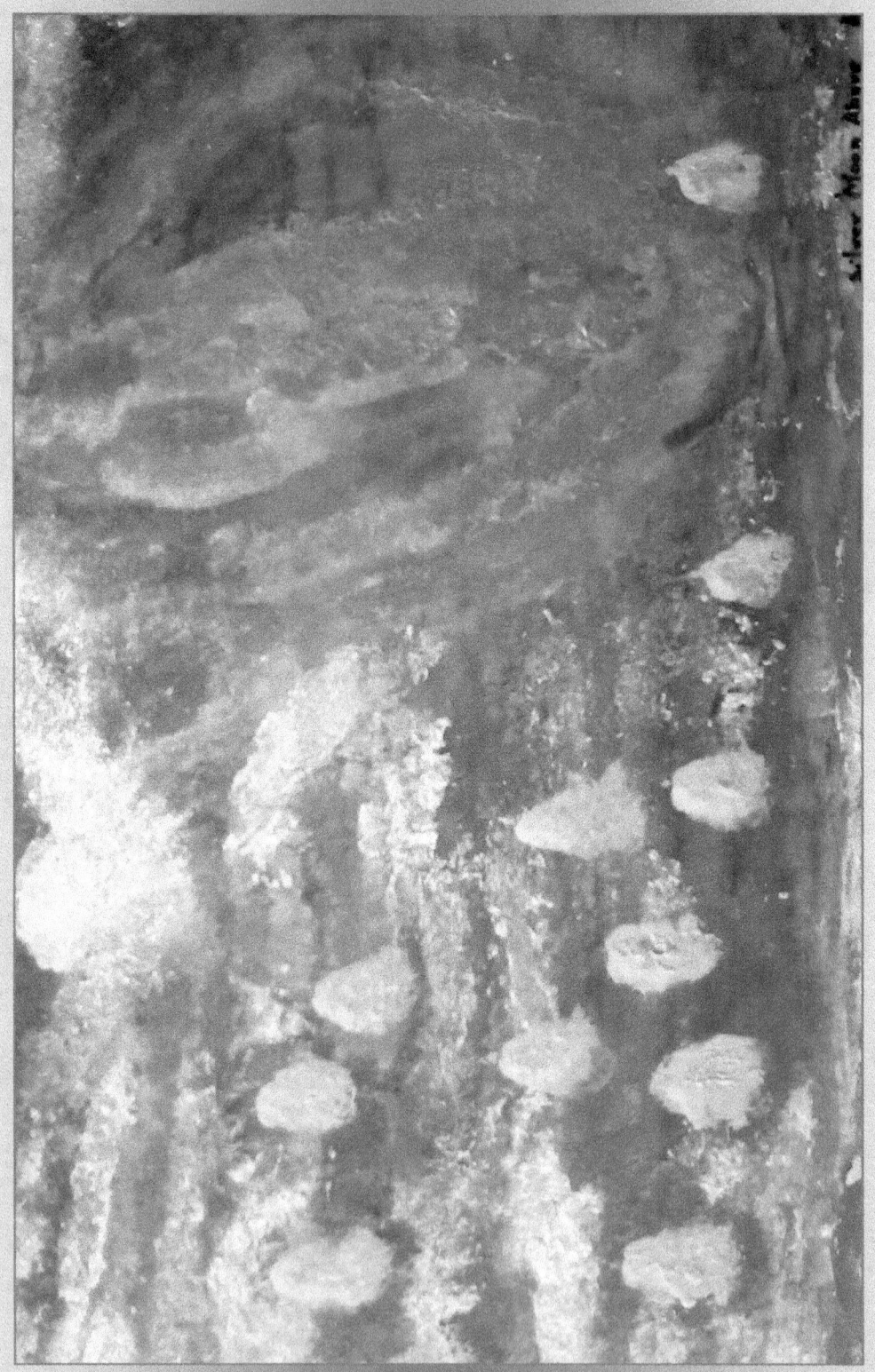
Silver Moon Above

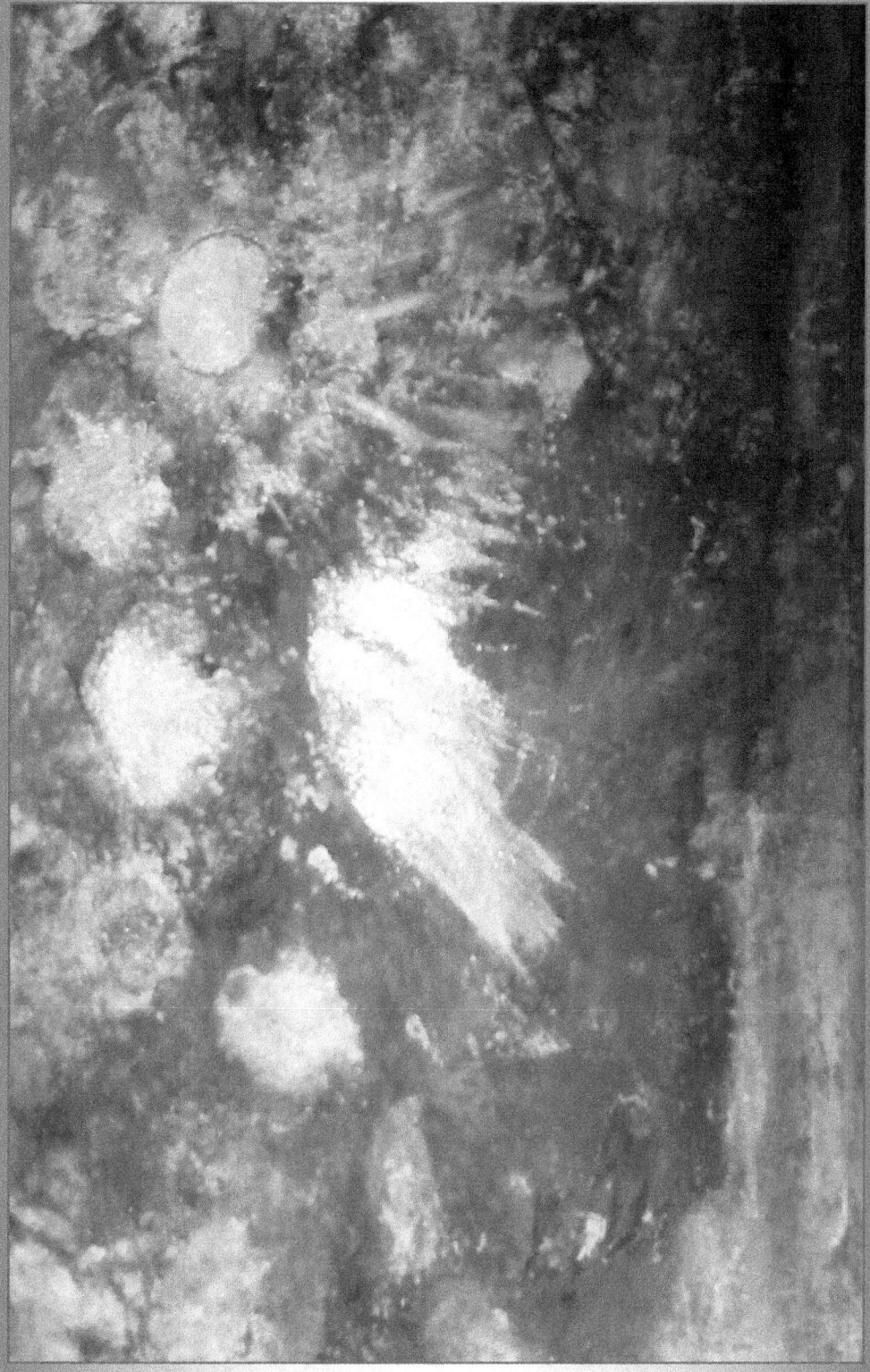

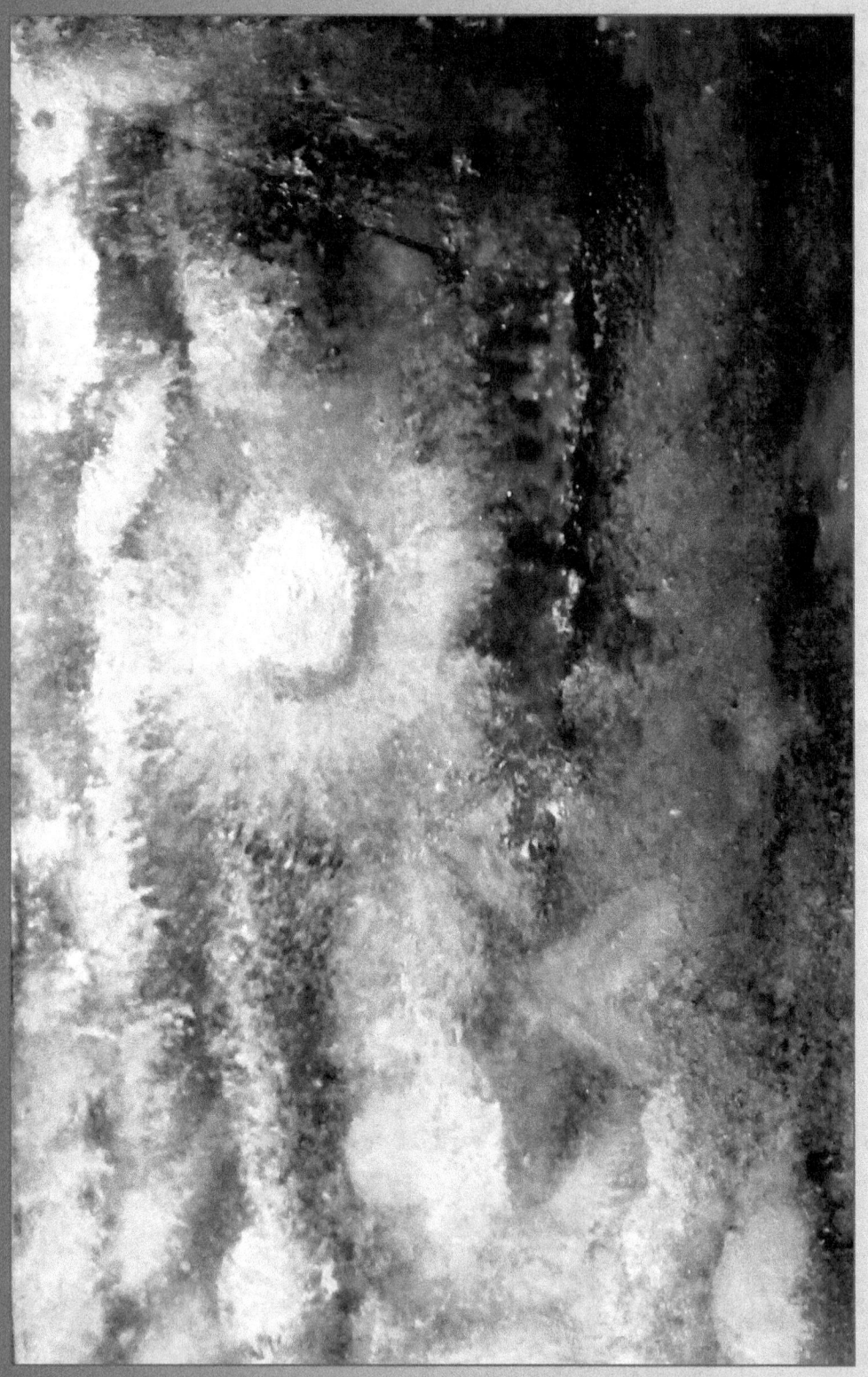

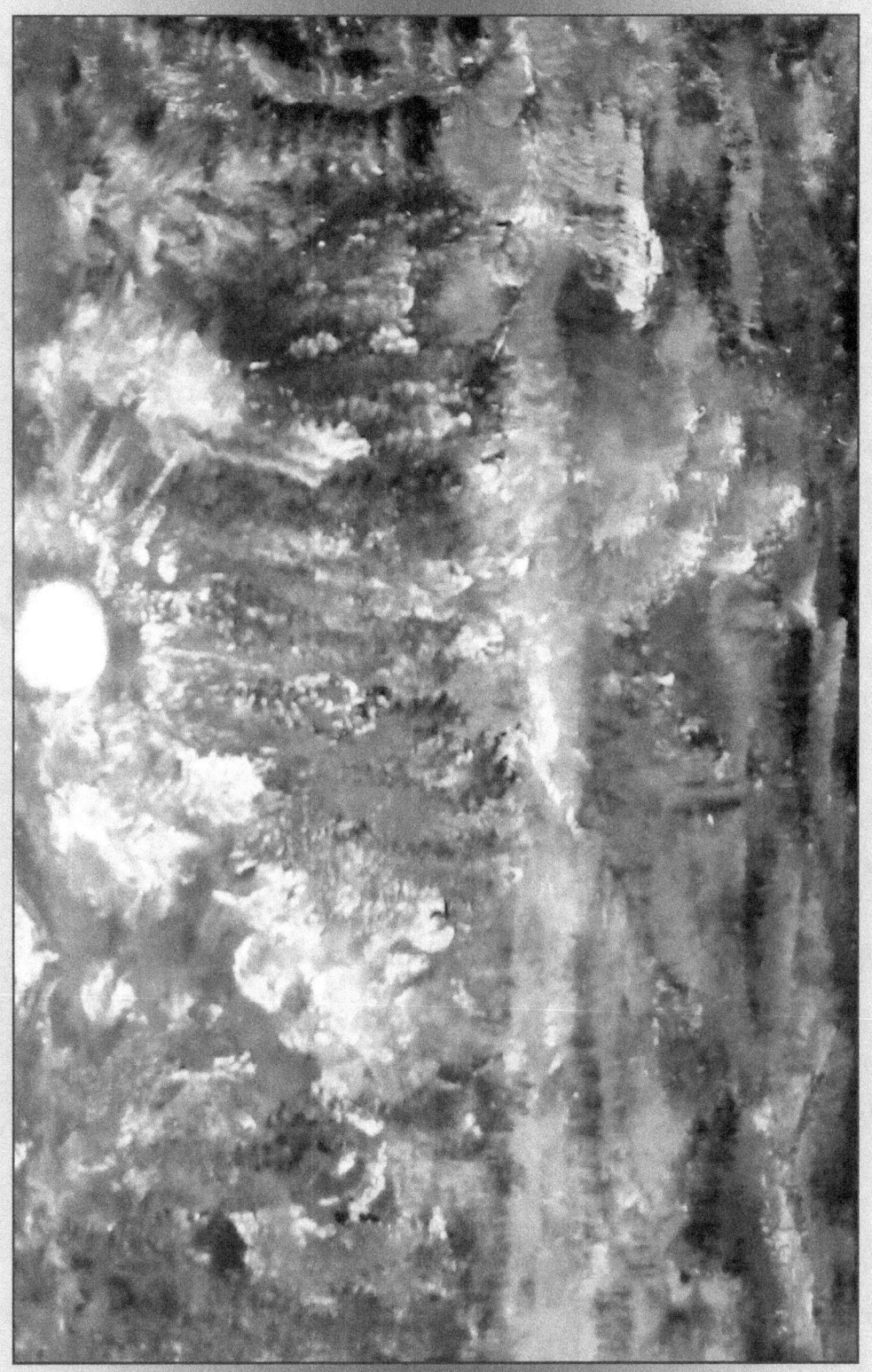

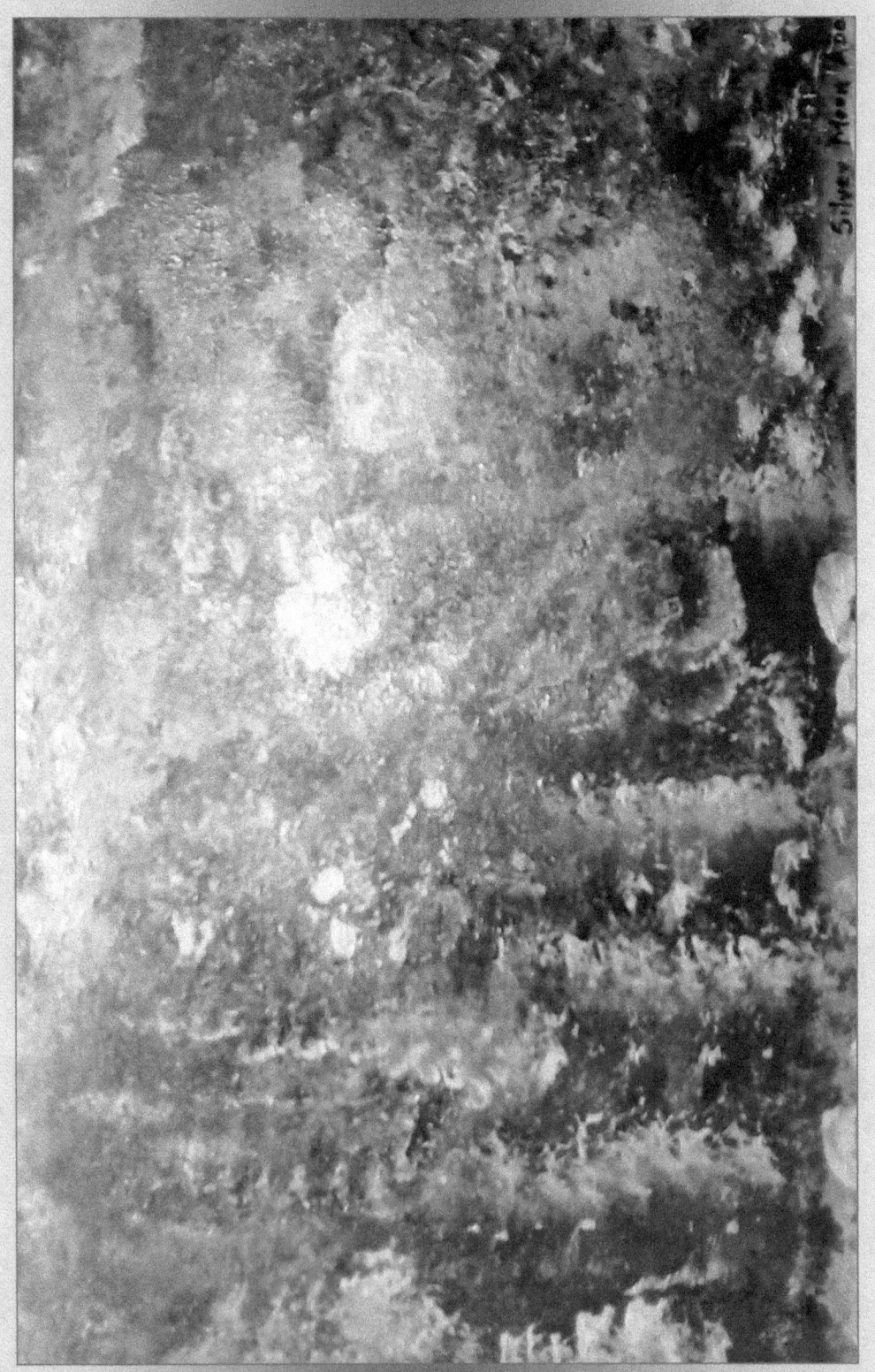

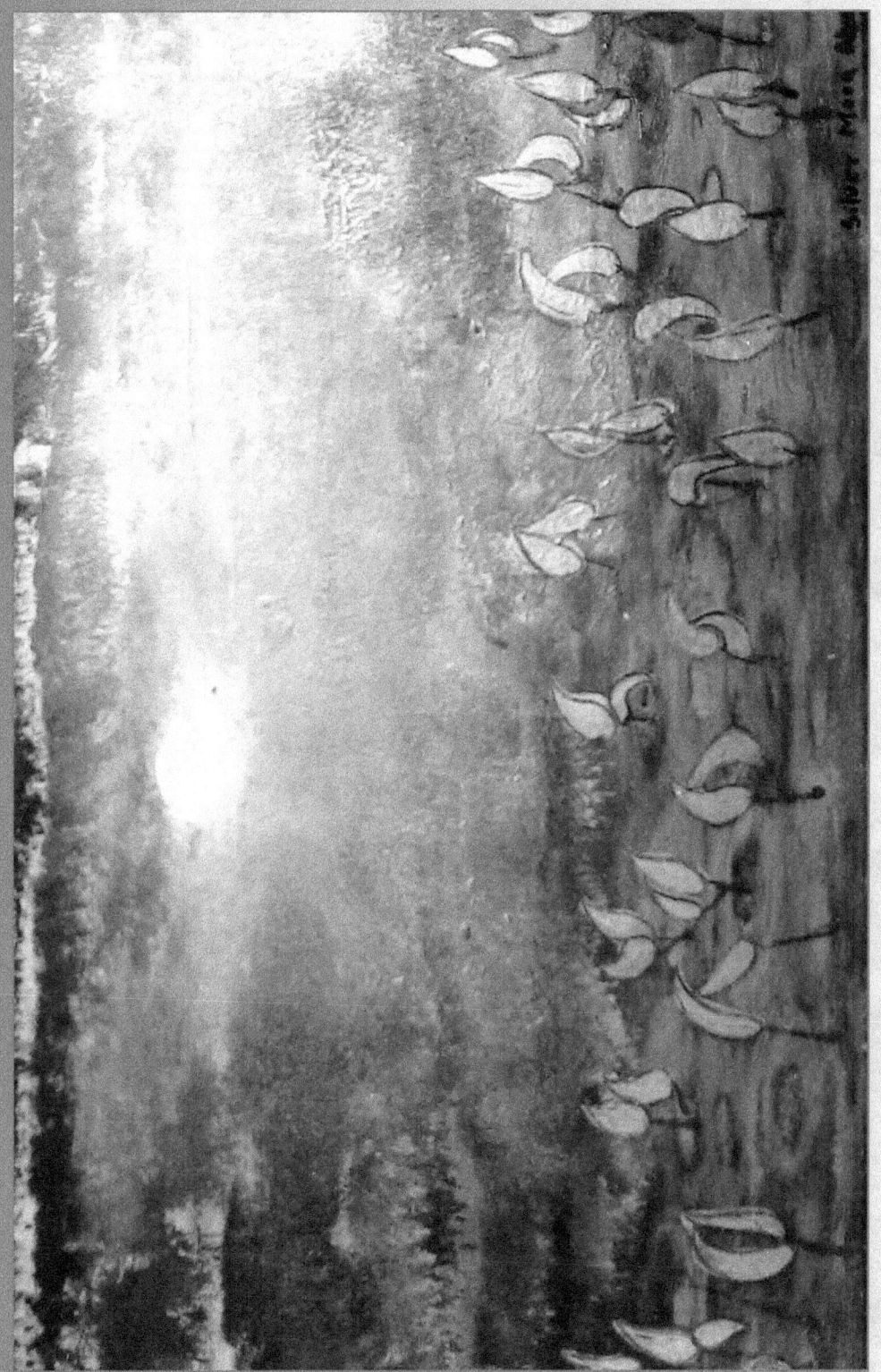

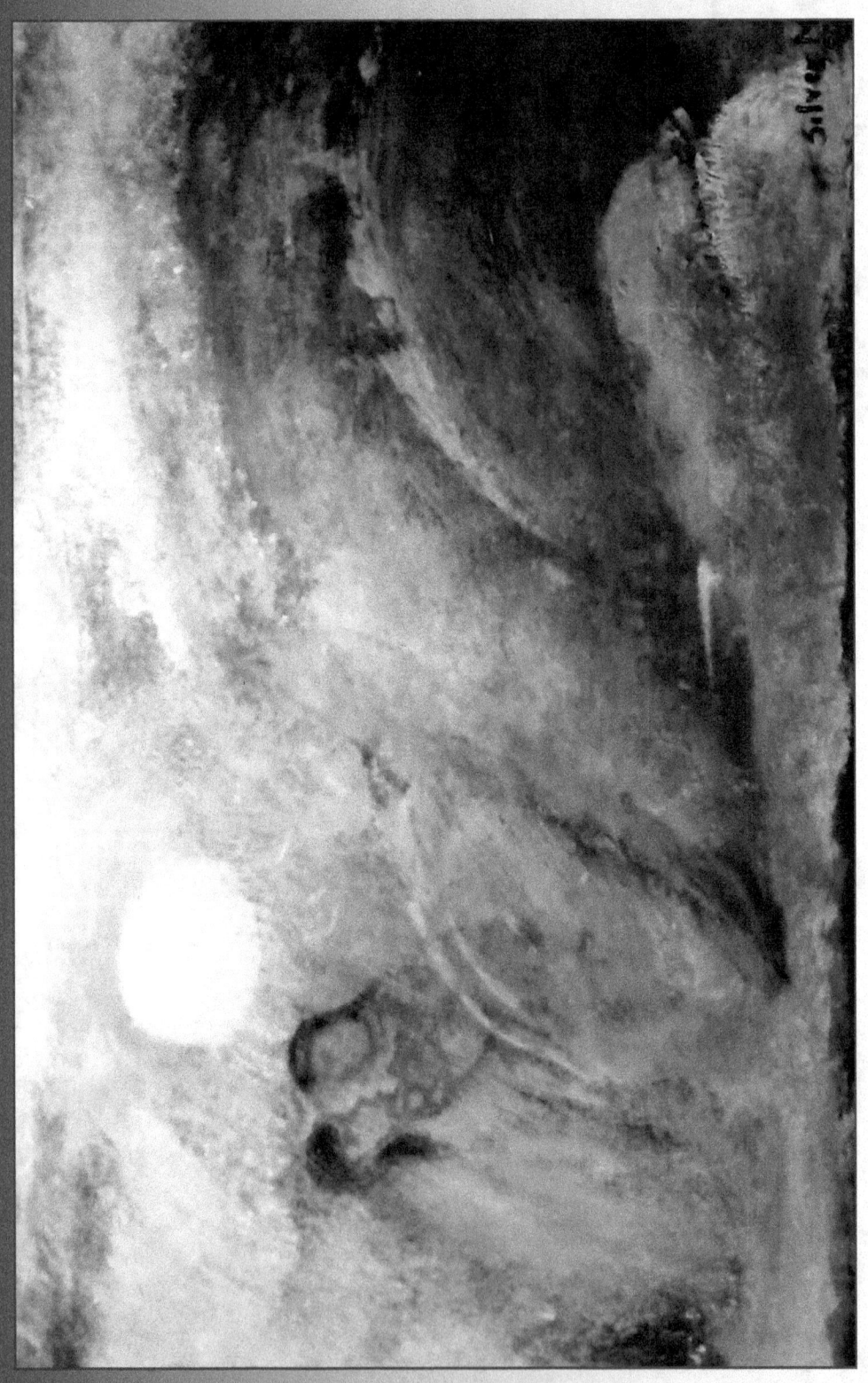

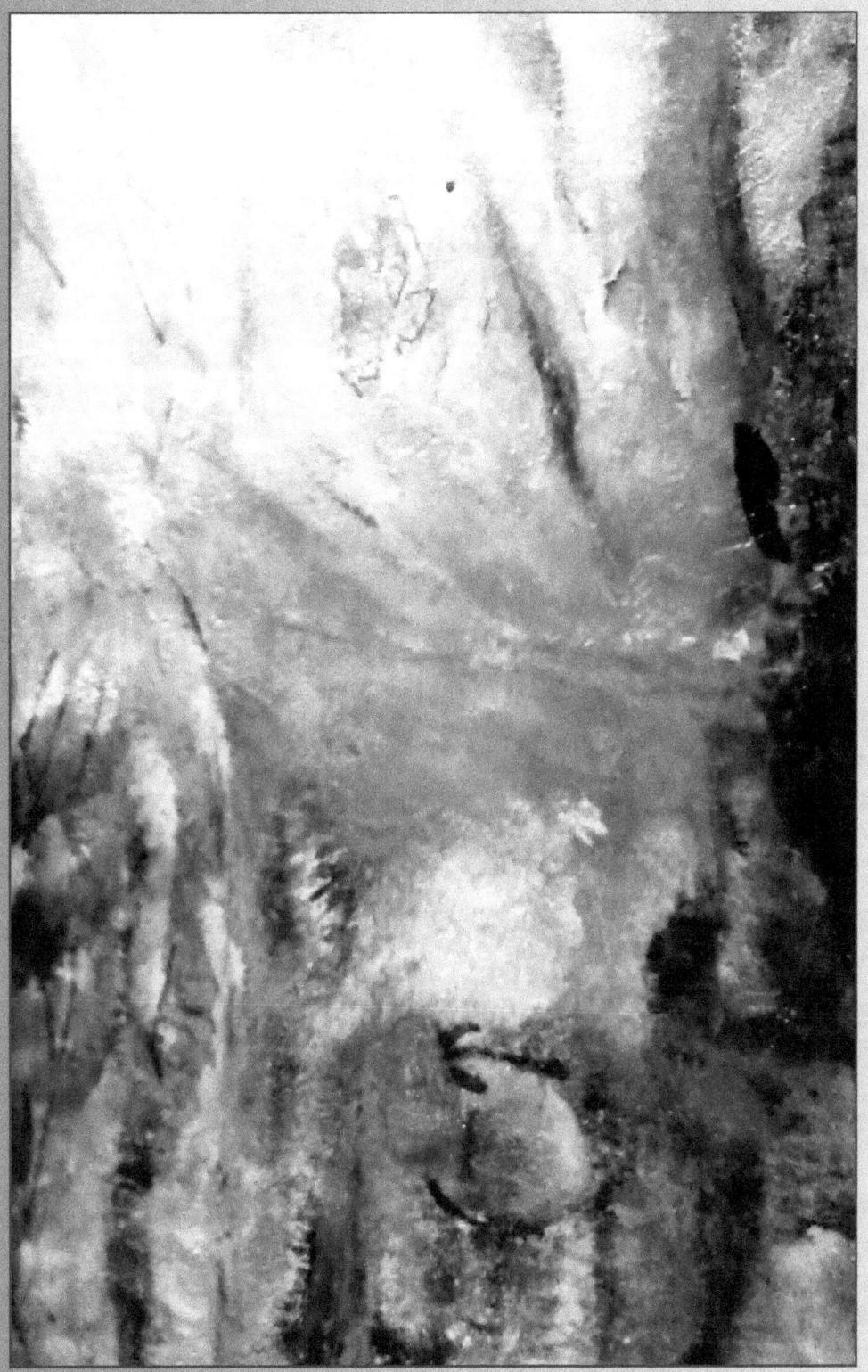

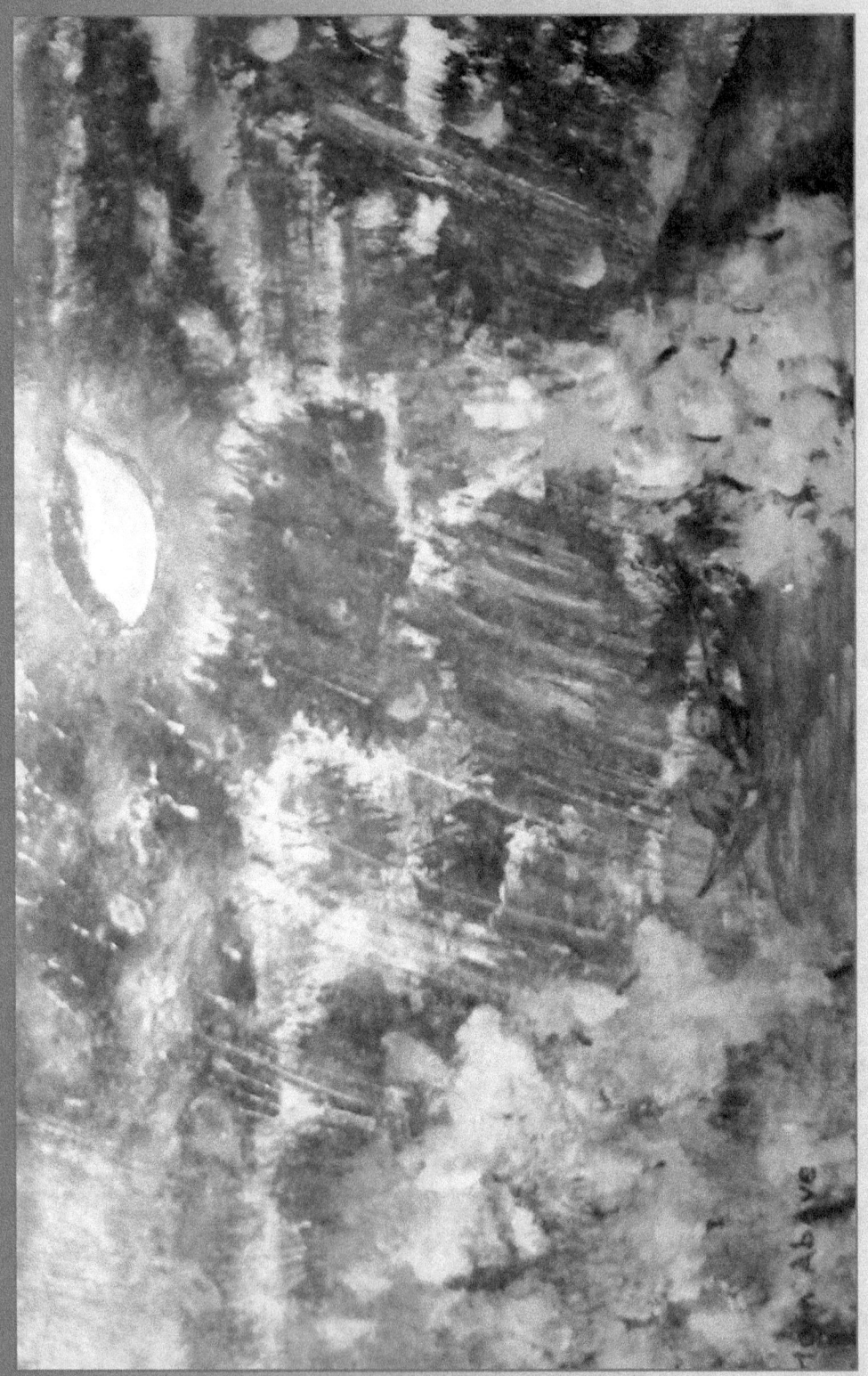

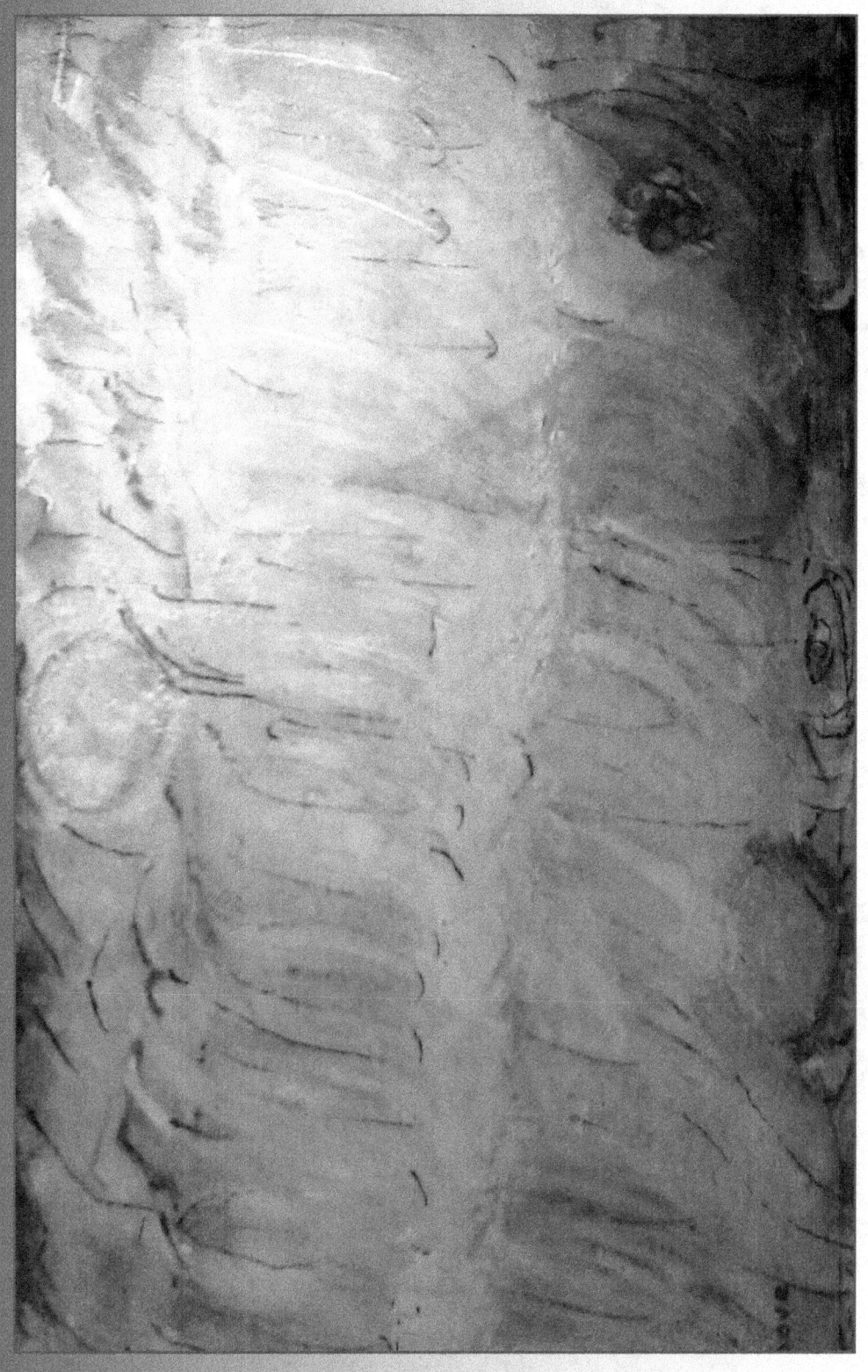

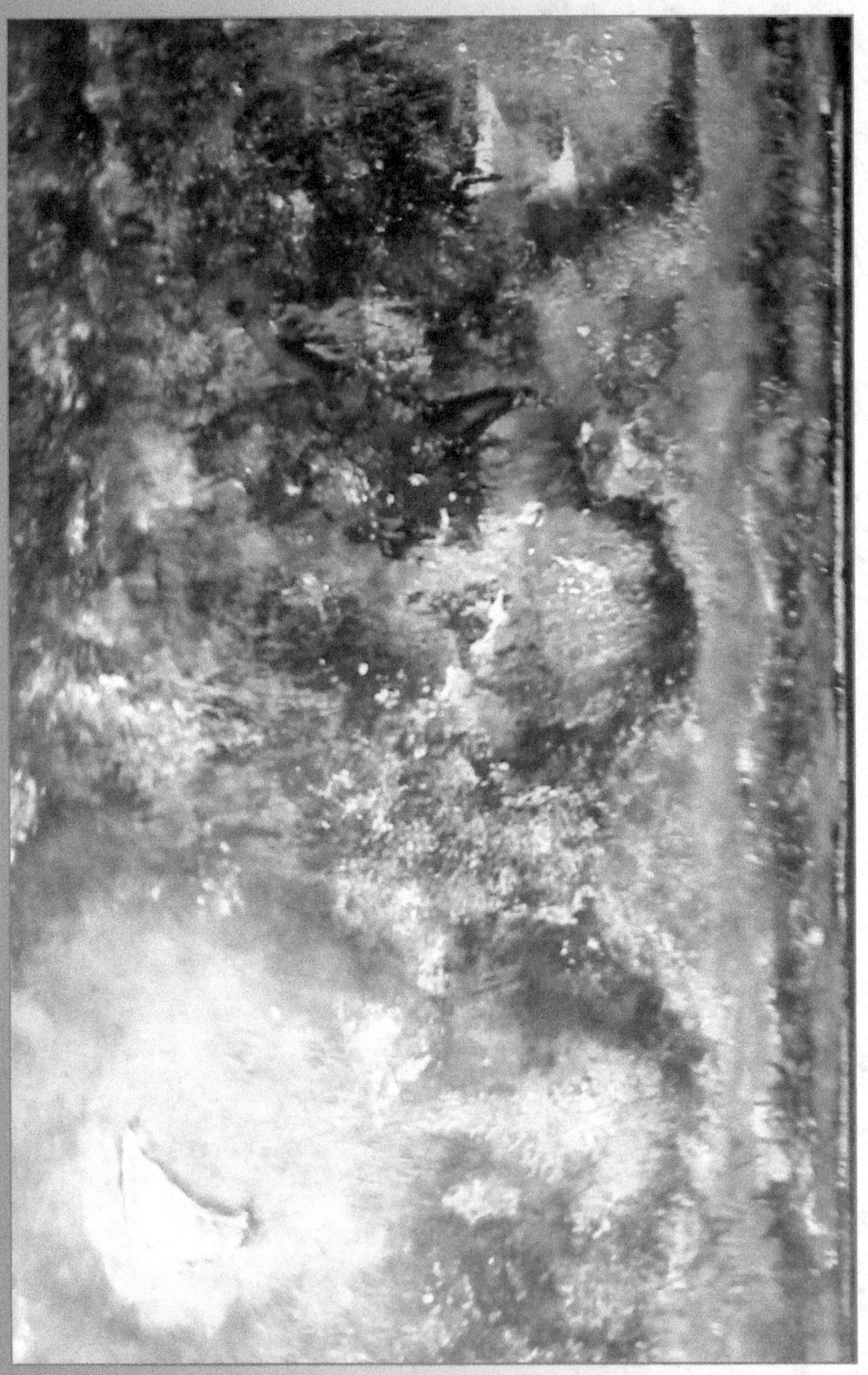

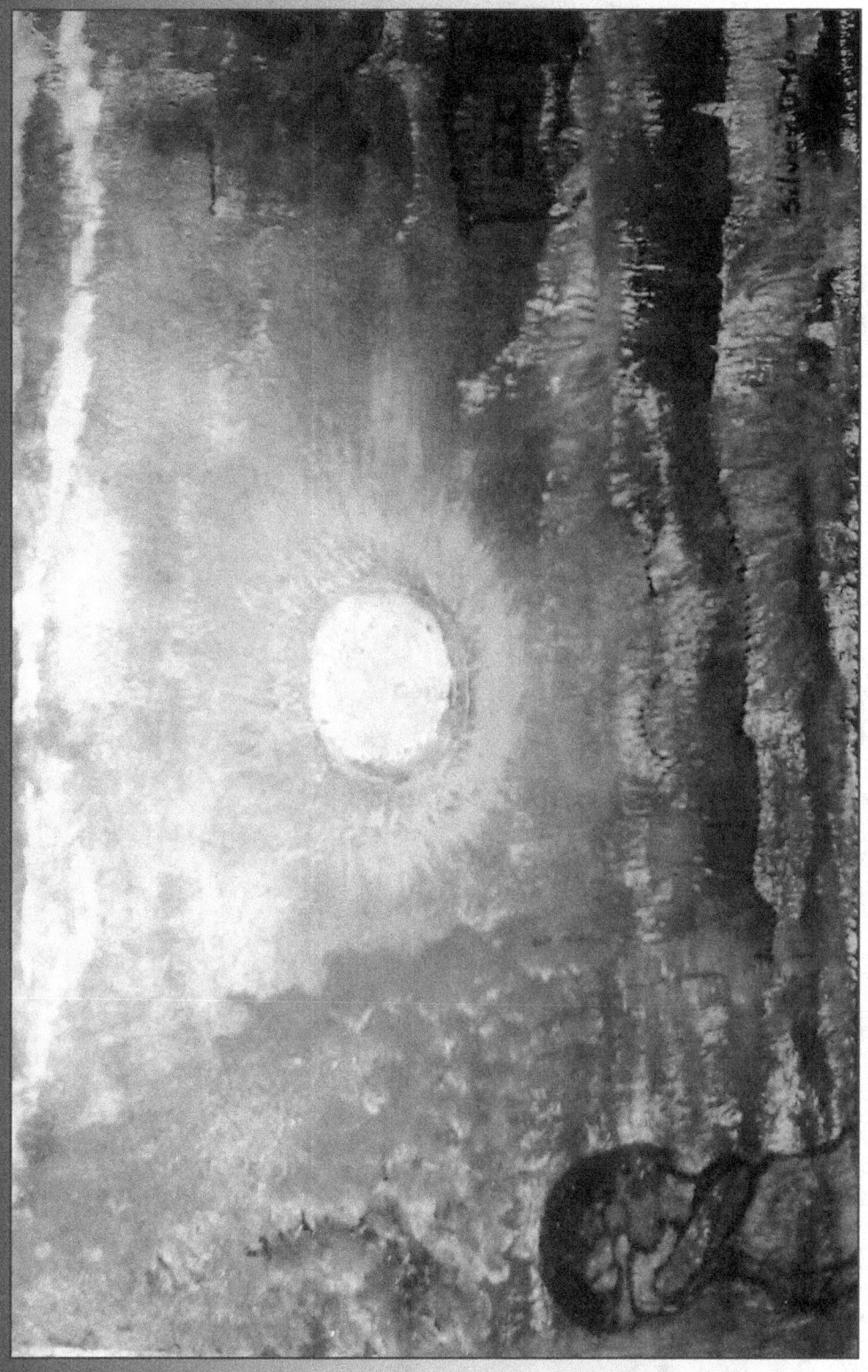

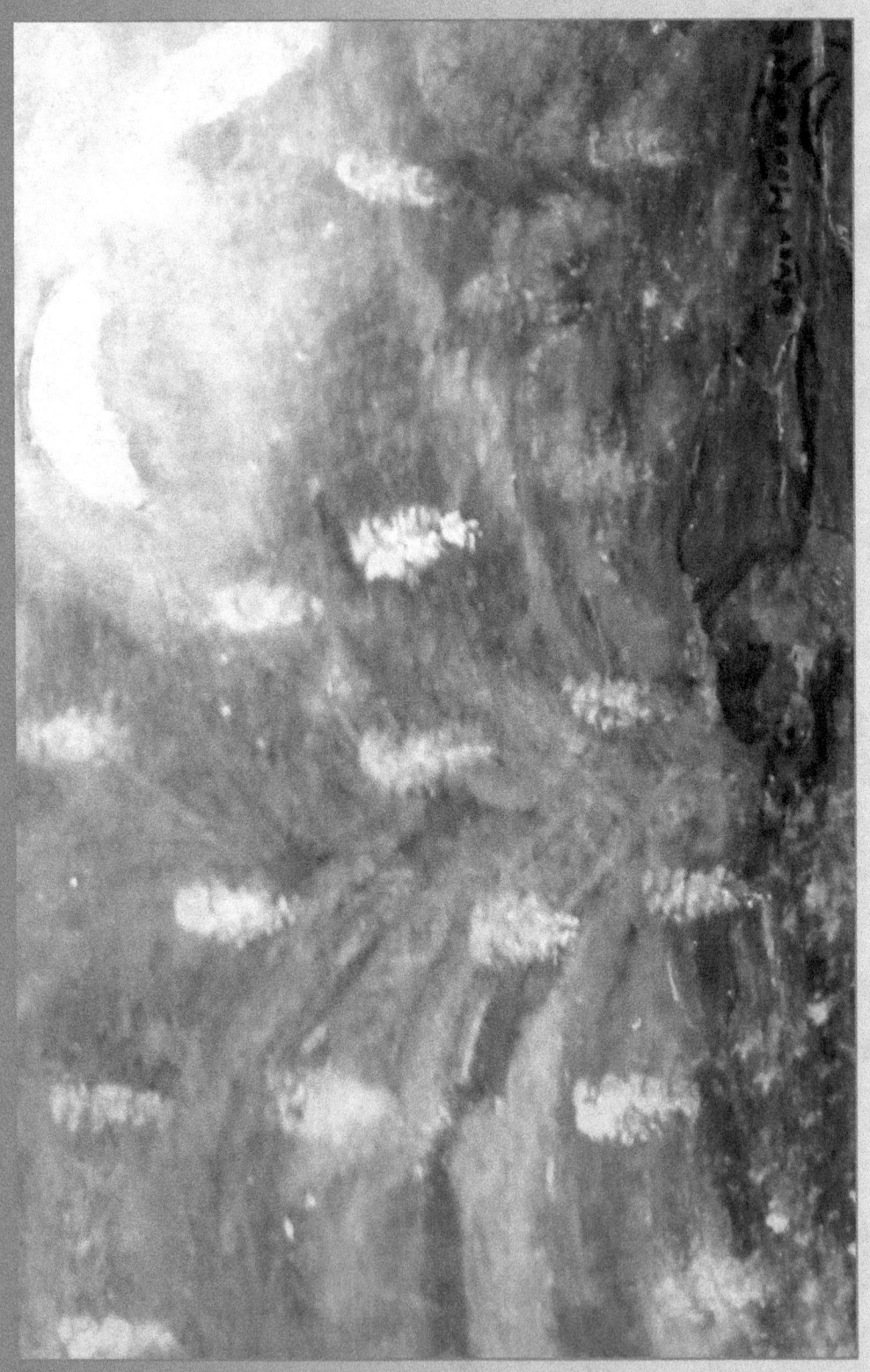

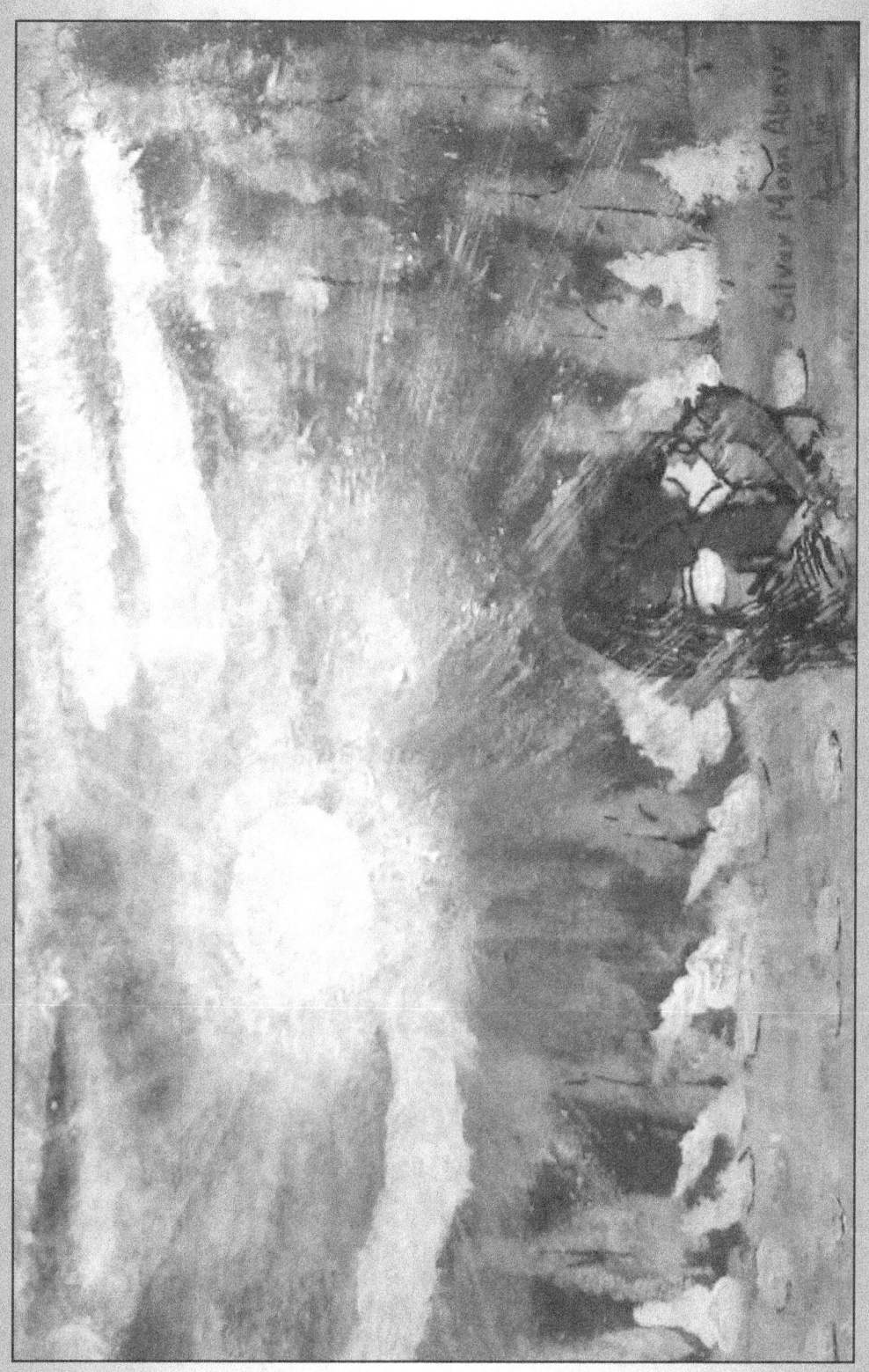

Silver Moon Above

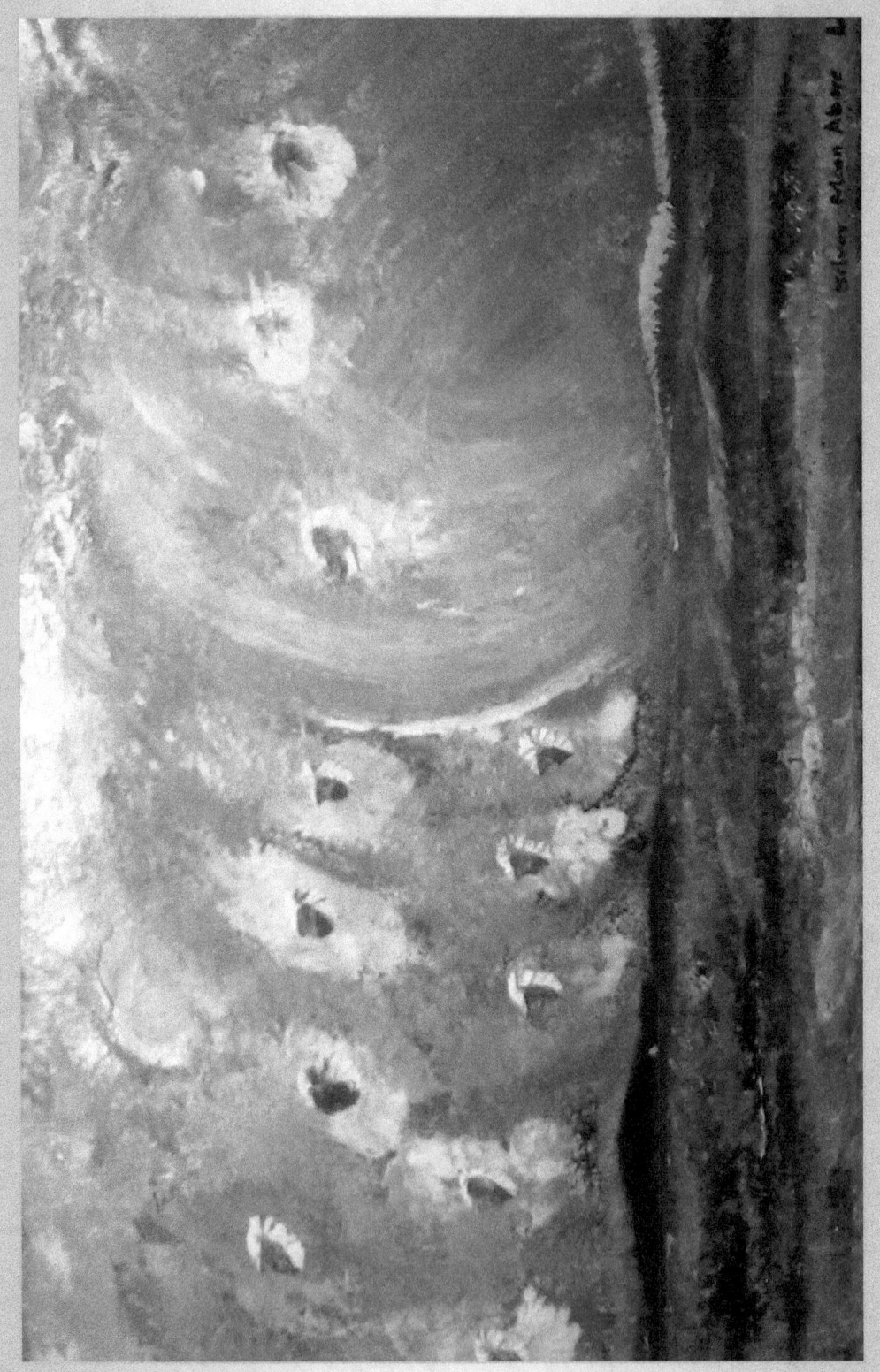

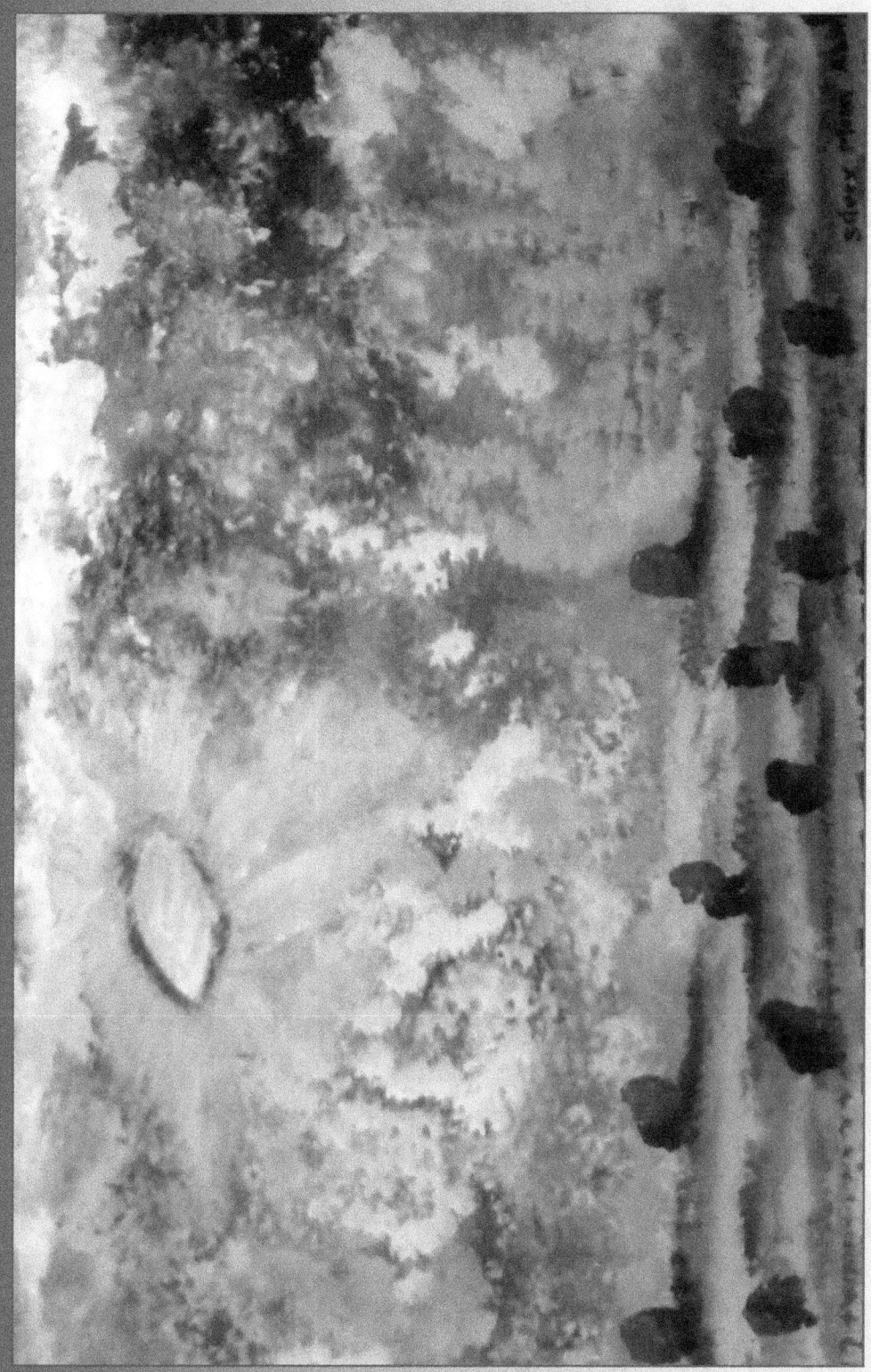

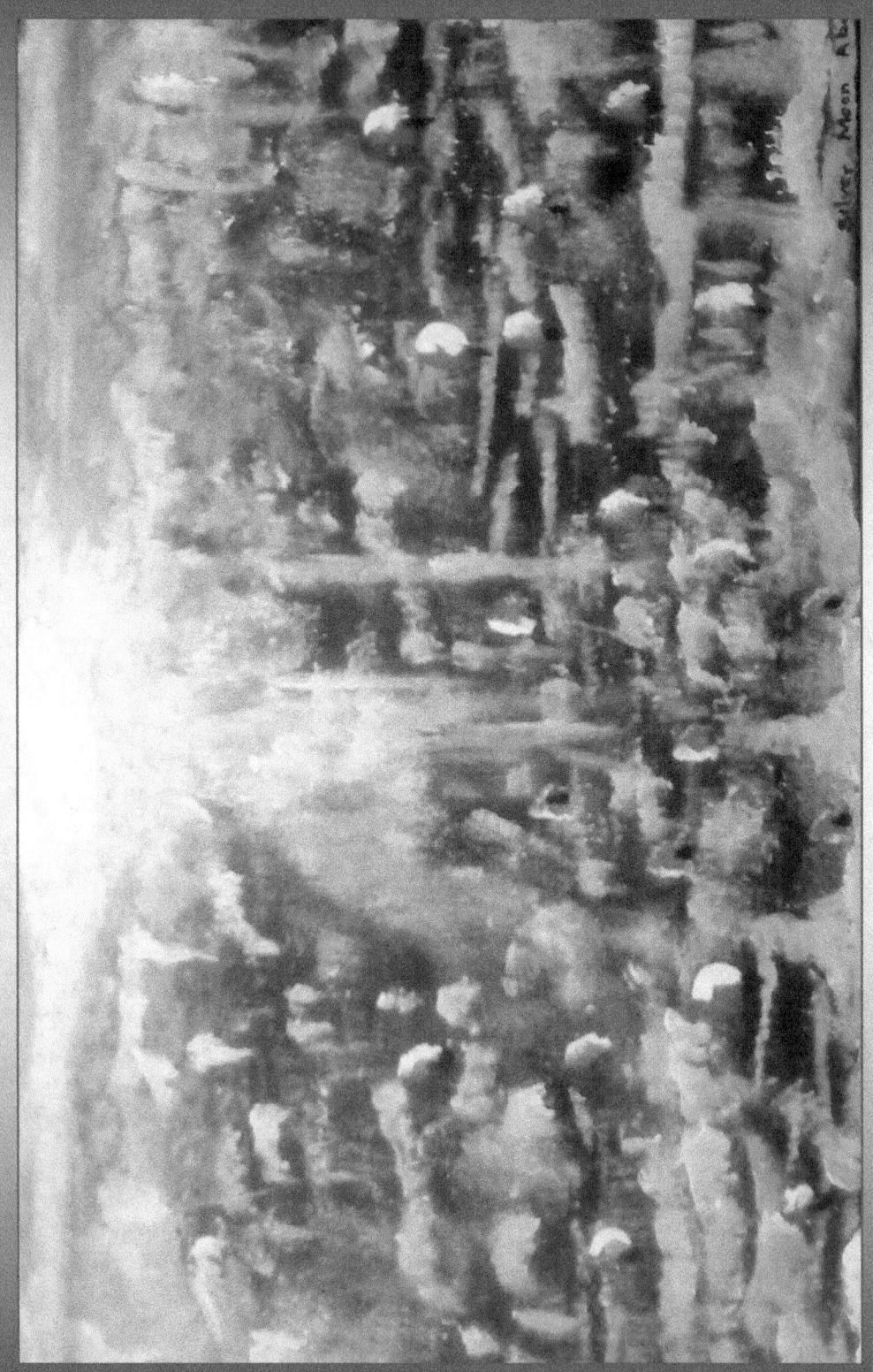

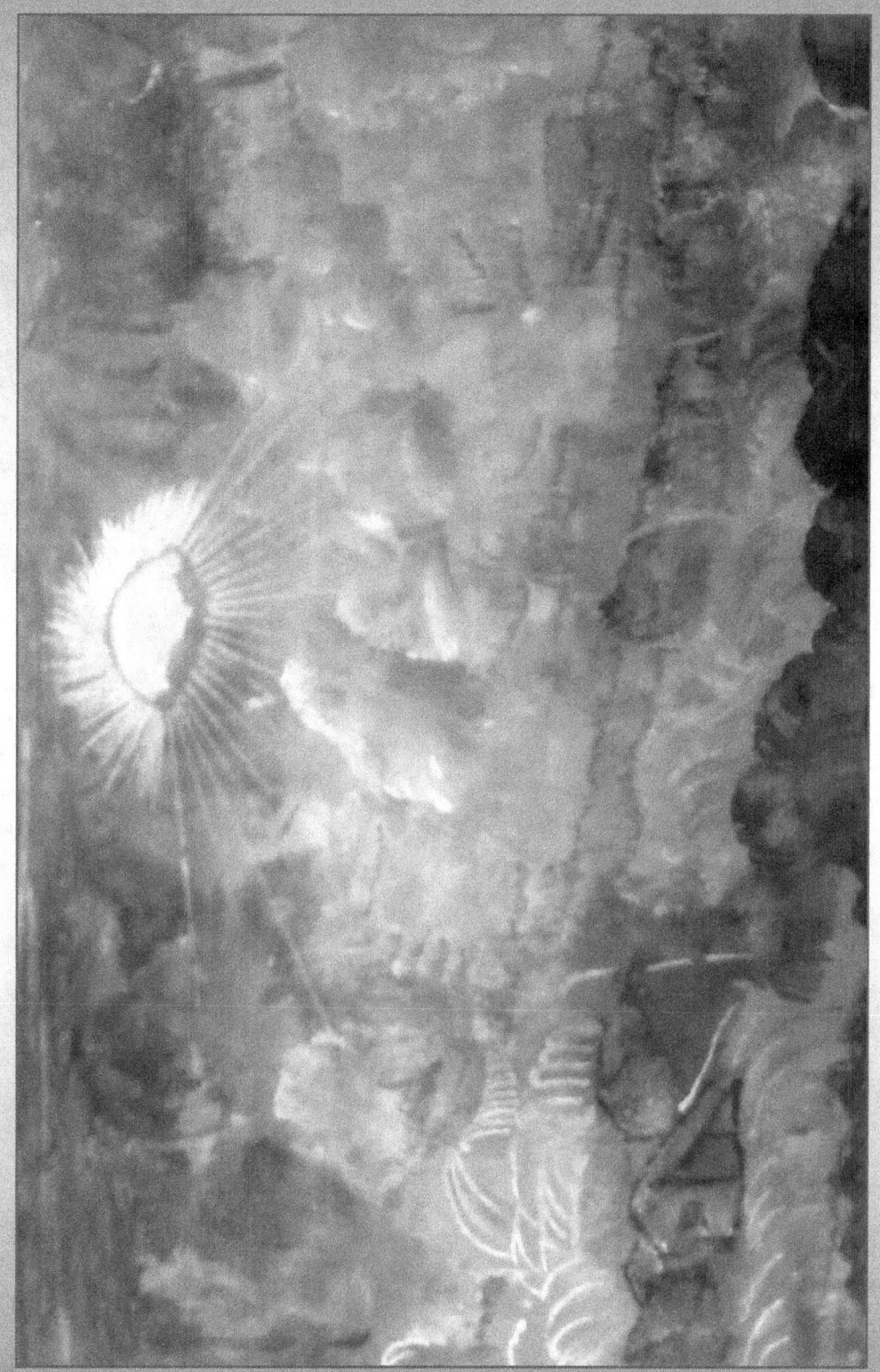

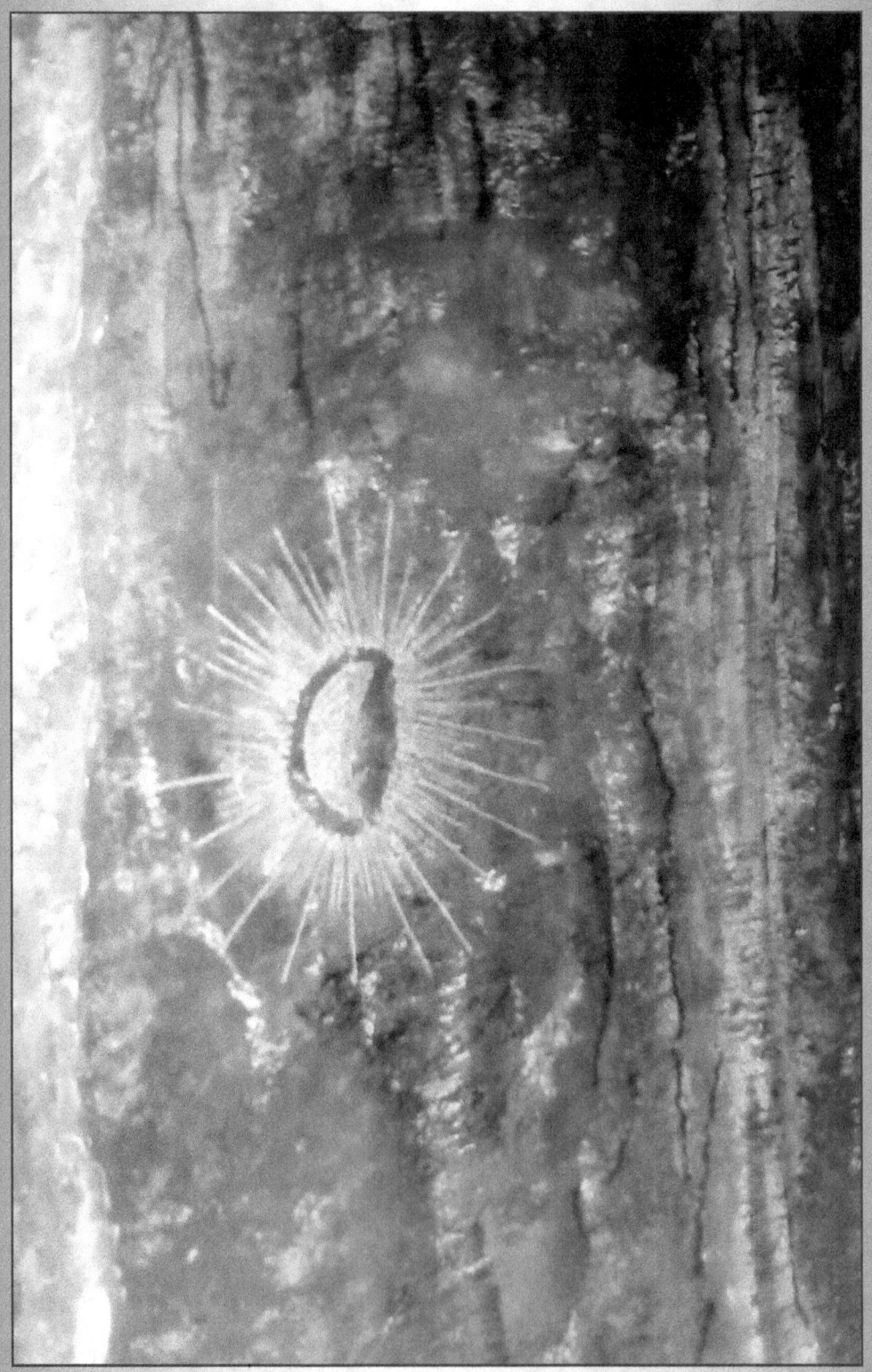

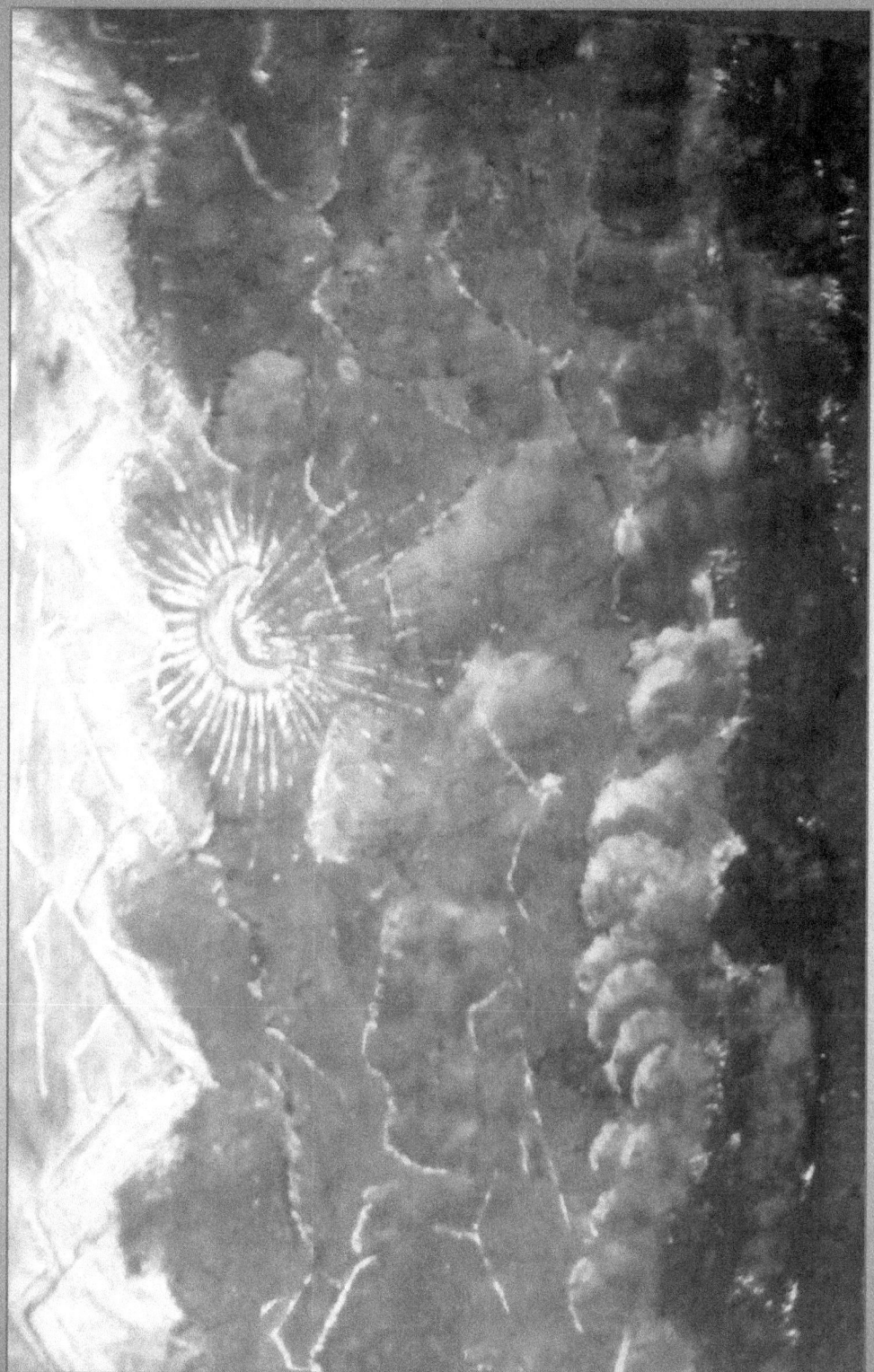

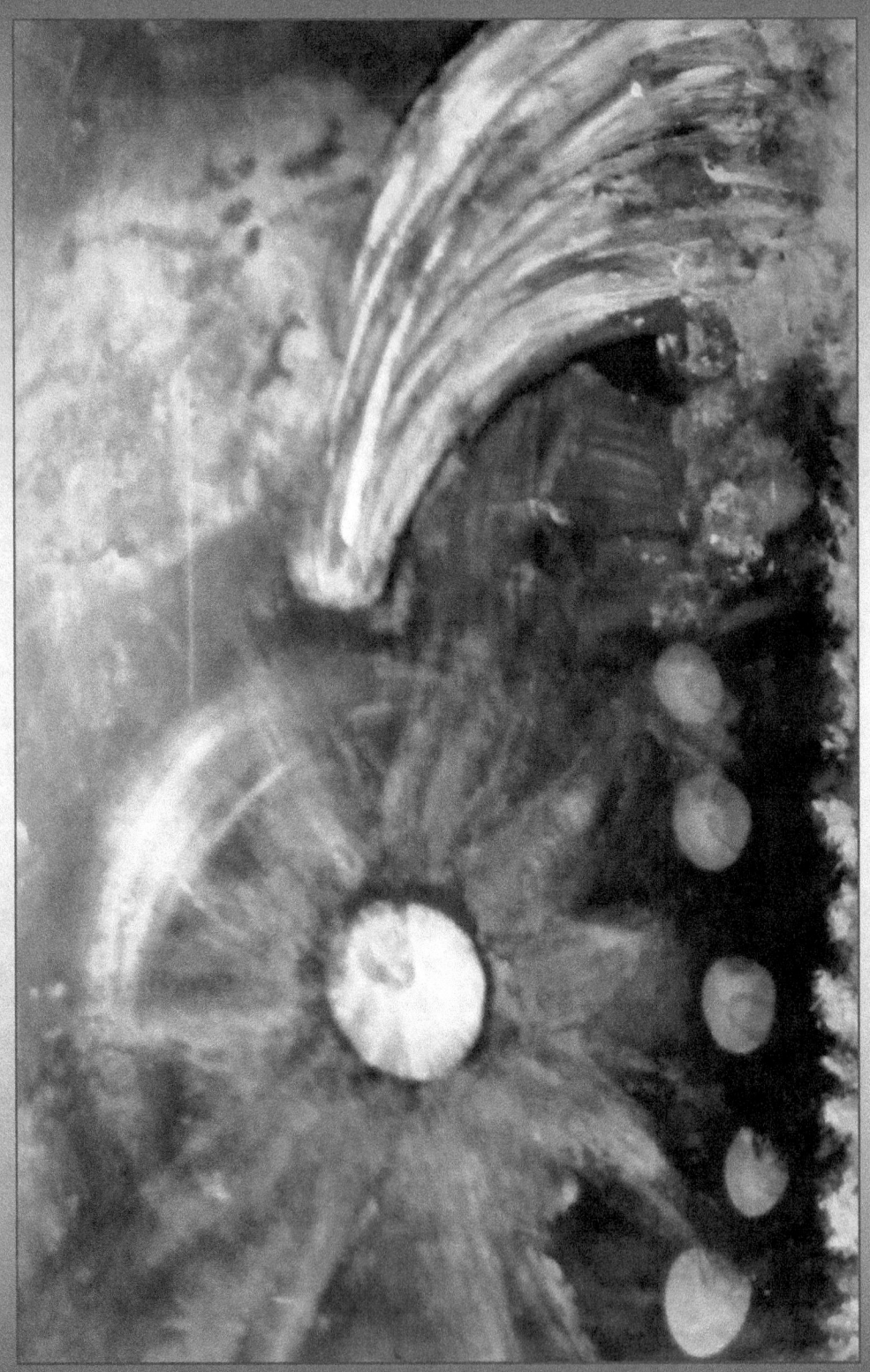

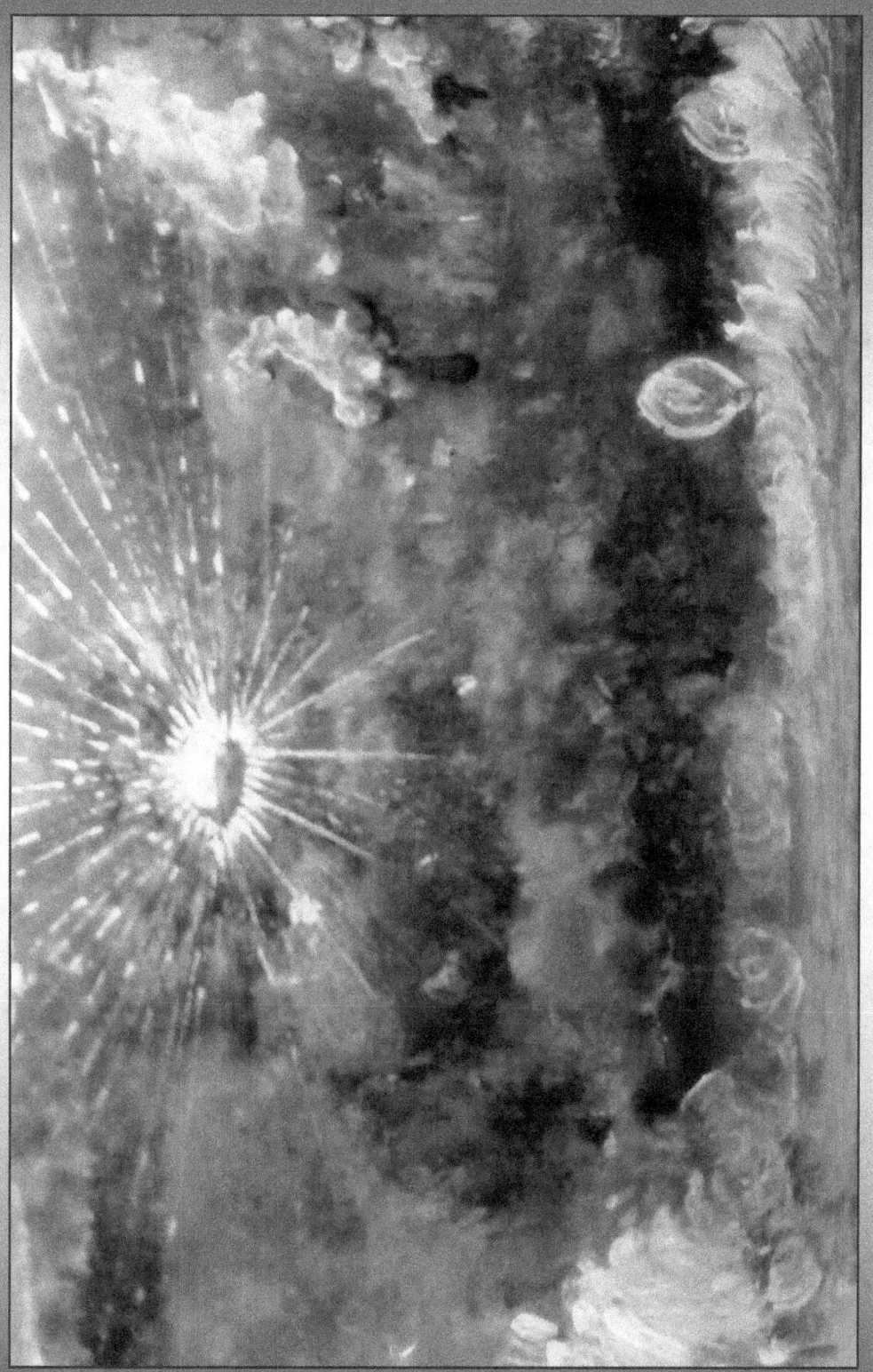

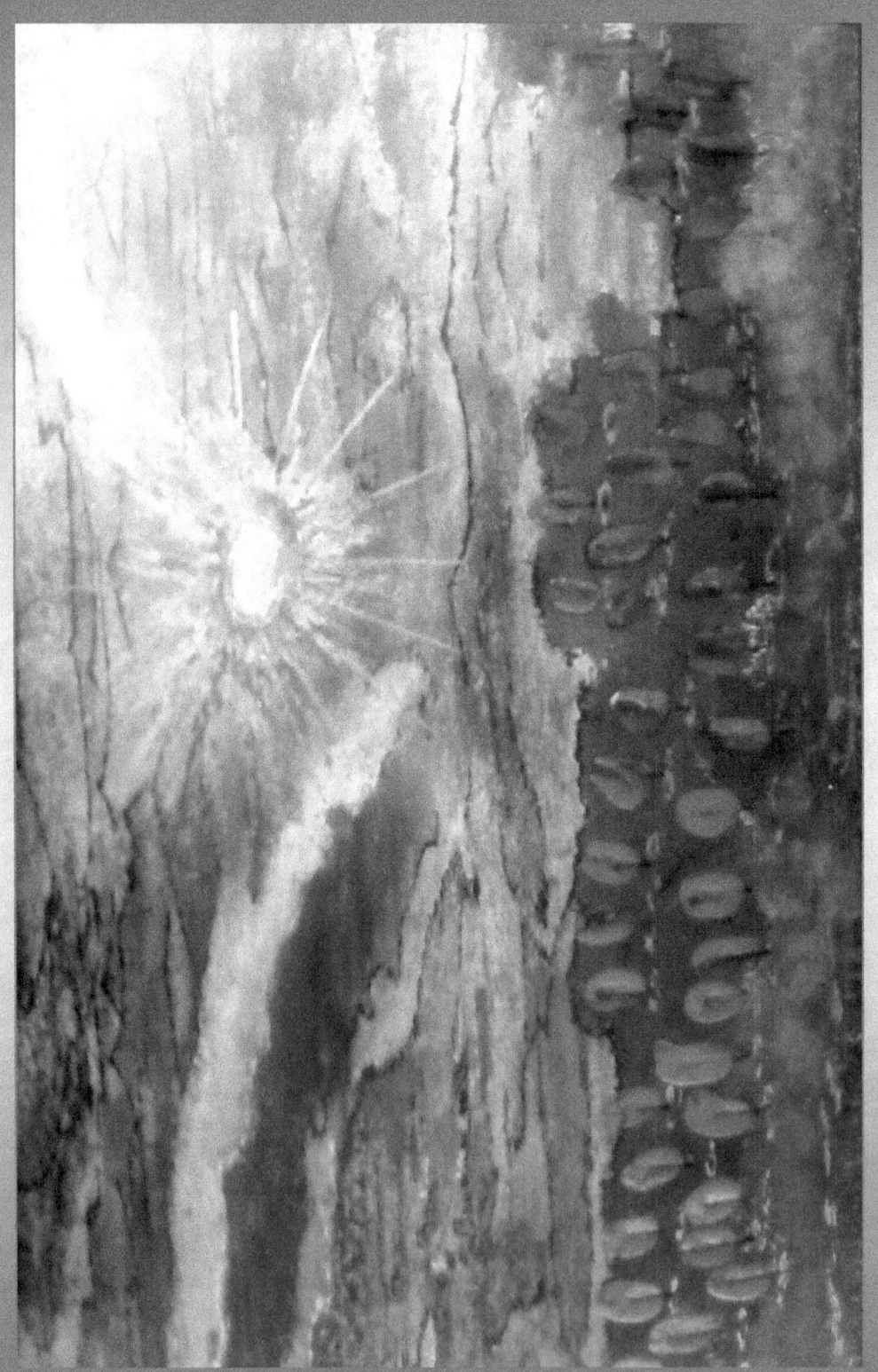

www.ingramcontent.com/pod-product-compliance
Lightning Source LLC
Chambersburg PA
CBHW081314180526
45170CB00007B/2698